F _ . _ . . . u

YELLOW

"Reader, beware, for *Flying Yellow* is not an easy path to follow. That's because these poems are, thankfully, nothing like the flat, prosaic landscape disguised as poetry today. Rhodes's is a deeply spiritual terrain, a book of many journeys with a voice who leads us like Dante's, meeting us in the deep woods 'with no way to know [what] will lead us out.' In these dark times, these poems of journey and survival are the 'flying yellow' day we need."

    —BRUCE GUERNSEY, author of *From Rain: Poems 1970-2010*

"This is one of the richest poetry collections I have read in a long time. Here are the intense images of a 1960s childhood, vivid narratives of family stresses and joys, and a panoply of voices—from colonial American women to a very pregnant Mary. These poems excite the spirit with revelations of the holy that one encounters in the most unlikely places, which of course is where the holy often appears."

    —JILL PELÁEZ BAUMGAERTNER, Poetry Editor, *The Christian Century*

"I have been reading and returning to Suzanne Underwood Rhodes's poems for twenty-five years—as bulwark, as shelter, for their attentiveness to the beauties of language, for their persistent opening into grace—and now comes *Flying Yellow*, like a gift from a wise friend that arrives when most needed. Rhodes is at the height of her strength here, life-affirming, generous, and precise, a voice with work to do in the world and in the spirit."

    —JAMES OWENS, poet, author of *Mortalia*

"From a childhood world 'torn / from things you'd think / shouldn't touch a child' to an adulthood carved into wisdom, 'after the sun drops / and the crickets have drawn their bows,' Rhodes gathers up things alongside the absence of things, in a defiant affirmation of blessedness. Throughout *Flying Yellow*, her unfailing attention to detail and exquisite language compel us to see in 'sunbursts or gray solemnity' and 'always / a heaven in view.' By the time we arrive at the closing poem, we know we have been offered something akin to 'the gold / of afterlife,' a God-infused reality—at times sorrowful, yet forever redeemed. *Flying Yellow* is salvific poetry at its most reverent, a crucial blessed antidote for our irreverent world."

—SOFIA STARNES, Virginia Poet Laureate, Emerita,
and author of *The Consequence of Moonlight*

"Once in a very long while, a voice reaches out to haunt you. Here, in an American idiom we can follow and trust, Suzanne Rhodes manages to reveal a Presence that lives within and beyond us. In poem after poem after poem, she shows us a broken world which, resurrected, can flame out in a music which, even as it burns, lifts us into a liminal space beyond anything we might ever have expected."

—PAUL MARIANI, University Professor Emeritus at Boston College,
poet and biographer

"In *Flying Yellow*, Suzanne Underwood Rhodes offers readers a collection that ranges from the homely holiness of everyday details to a figurative richness that edges quietly toward transcendence. Her diction is plain but precise, her attention to sound unfailing, her syntax consistently rhythmic and controlled. Despite their span of subject and form, these poems are bound together by a tacit pattern as mysterious as it is sure."

—WILLIAM JOLLIFF, Contributing Editor, *The Windhover*,
and author of *Twisted Shapes of Light*

FLYING

NEW AND
SELECTED
POEMS

To Margaret,
a poet I much admire
and now a friend.
May your pilgrimage
in faith and art
lead to deeper
knowledge of
the Holy.
Suzanne Underwood Rhodes

YELLOW

SUZANNE
UNDERWOOD
RHODES

PARACLETE PRESS
BREWSTER, MASSACHUSETTS

for Wayne, gentlest presence

for my children, Katy, Stephen and Emily

and for Larry, my dear friend and best critic

2021 First Printing

Flying Yellow: New and Selected Poems

Copyright © 2021 by Suzanne Underwood Rhodes

ISBN 978-1-64060-402-5

The Paraclete Press name and logo (dove on cross) are trademarks of Paraclete Press

Library of Congress Cataloging-in-Publication Data
Names: Rhodes, Suzanne U., 1950- author.
Title: Flying yellow : new and selected poems / Suzanne Underwood Rhodes.
Description: Brewster, Massachusetts : Paraclete Press, [2021] | Summary:
 "A hopeful belief in heaven and the end of suffering colors these
 profoundly spiritual, often uneasy, poems"-- Provided by publisher.
Identifiers: LCCN 2020047615 (print) | LCCN 2020047616 (ebook) | ISBN
 9781640604025 (trade paperback) | ISBN 9781640604032 (mobi) | ISBN
 9781640604049 (epub) | ISBN 9781640604056 (pdf)
Subjects: LCGFT: Poetry.
Classification: LCC PS3568.H665 F59 2021 (print) | LCC PS3568.H665
 (ebook) | DDC 811/.54--dc23
LC record available at https://lccn.loc.gov/2020047615
LC ebook record available at https://lccn.loc.gov/2020047616

10 9 8 7 6 5 4 3 2 1

Published by Paraclete Press
Brewster, Massachusetts
www.paracletepress.com

Printed in the United States of America

. . . flesh is but the glasse which holds the dust
That measures all our time . . .
—George Herbert in "Church-Monuments"

CONTENTS

I

II

III

IV

I

Radiance

My mother is drying her hair
in the yard by the pink-feathered mimosa.
Betty Grable's legs never looked so good
as Mom's in short shorts, swung
to one side of the lawn chair.
She's wearing the sleeveless blouse
I ironed for her in the damp
basement of the overflowing basket,
happy to bring her things to light.

Most days, stories and poems from her hand
overruled the laundry, outlived
my stepfather's complaint,
and his ashes.

I'm thirteen and moved to write a poem
about her, my queen,
not seeing she'd grow bald
from sickness, seeing only rubies
catch fire in her comb.

At her feet lies the coiled garden hose.
She's closed her dreaming eyes, heavy with sun.
I'm watching from a space between
curtains to let the words alight,
let the eyes on the wings feast
on her radiant hair.

A Theme Perhaps for the Plague

It is the memory of your harmonies and the grim house
lifting in your ebullience that I'm holding against
this deadly fugue, the flight from everything and nothing
we the world have known.

I would be singing somewhere in the house
and you'd come streaming into the song,
your strong alto current bearing my higher notes
into joy that was, I see now, a resistance

against the rage smoldering within those walls
as you found the balancing notes from an inward spring.
How good to think of that now as I stir soup
inside my home holding strong from what's outside.

My Mother Haunts the Thrift Store

When I saw the glint of her French hoop earrings as she lighted the steps
of the bus taking her downtown to a job that stoked my stepfather's ire,
her ponytail high and swinging, the envy of the other office girls,
saw the ghost of those hoops in the cracked display case of pop-beads
and bangles, and the same cloisonné heart given her by my sister
who sleeps far away but weeps in faded pages of my mother's journal—
and then, down the aisles, rack after rack, the coral, the aqua, the striking
white on black—color was her flair, her strong opinions shaming pale shirts
of thought (but oh, what heads she turned with those colors!). When I
passed the books packed tight on sinking shelves, and spied among
the hot-throated covers of cheap paperbacks, biographies of John Adams
and Charlemagne, a King James Bible, Truman Capote novels following her
through many moves and two dead husbands to feed her restless mind,
the mind that fed me, too, all the way back to gypsies and poets singing
in books she read to me in sheltered spaces. When I came to the shoes,
high heels announcing her long, shapely legs, those suede shoes I longingly
brushed as she dressed for an evening out, the complex glamour
of her French twist and mystical air of Chanel No. 5, the sorrow
of her true red lipstick—all this transfixed me with the force of a dream
I still reach for, and even the linens, the sheets and spreads bleached clean
of love and death, speak of her body so present in everything given away.

How the Dress Lived

"The creative mind plays with the objects it loves" —*Carl Jung*

Like my mother, I unmade clothes to make them.
It was a war between rules and resistance
to see how far we could get before conceding,
in the face of the wrong pocket,
to the pattern's authority.

For us, the making was all in the feeling,
the sewing from senses. I'd pin my moth-thin
pattern to the fabric cut
from a big, starchy bolt that landed
with a thump on the counter.
The salesgirl in glasses with a head for math
unrolled the reams of cloth and snipped
my yards and a half with her expert scissors,
its bite releasing denim's blue stiffness,
organza's gauzy pools

and then to go home and lay out my fabric,
seeing myself as the Butterick girl sketched
with goddess curves in the dress I was sewing
in colors of gold or teal to complement my hair—
to set up the Singer with its pinpoint light,
work the pedal, train the spool's thread to the bobbin
thrumming ever faster as I thought of my dress,
how gorgeous I'd be, like the girls at school
in stylish clothes from Garfinckel's.

"No, prettier," Mom would say
as she stood me on a chair to re-hem a skirt,
trusting her eye, not the tape measure,
with straight pins like defiant little spears
between her lips as she tucked and tugged,
nodding yes to the girl of her birthing,
cut from her own unruly swath to suit
the shapes, dreams, colors of her mind.

Needle in Curtain

Teensy dagger
fixed in lace,
my mother's needle
upended splinters
and mended loose buttons.
The kitchen curtains blew
it about, a silver glint
winking now in my kitchen
decades later,
the breezes still coming inside,
the needle still all-knowing
with its eye
on the wound
and the tear.

The Caricaturist

My first death I was riding in the backseat of the Buick Special
studying my stepfather's neck with its stitchwork of lines
when over the wind's rush from the downed windows
he announced, "Bill Fetters is dead."
My comic book slid from my lap because all I could think of
was Mr. Fetters sticking his hand in that fan at my parents' party
and blood flying around the room and Daddy explaining
it was for laughs, the crazy SOB, and now he was saying
he died of a pickled liver. I pictured the poor, gasping fish
and turned to drown my face in wind.

What parties!
They danced and drank in the basement
with its pole jacking up the house
to the throb of jazz on the hi-fi, a haze of cigars
and cocktail dresses, my mother with her chic French twist,
men with loose ties, and laughter roaring through the vents,
the adults in their fugitive world, and me and my sisters in ours,
free until two a.m., when the house came back from the party

and shrank to our dining room table
with its cracks between leaves,
where Daddy nailed his fools with a genius art,
knew their true colors with a devil's eye.

Secretly, I tried to let them out, poking at my lima beans
to offer Bill a backbone, Fritz hair, me a slim body,
light, a little more light in the lead-gray room
where Mommy was always excusing losers
when his words were stripping us, smiting the helpless lines.
She tried to make peace, a thin, watery soup

not good for much but more than the ashes
that came of his scorn, a scar deeper
than any I owned.

Incurable Chili

He shouts
from the cottage door,
shredding
the air's tree-woven
silence.

We come stumbling
down the rocks from our hideout
and snap-to at the table.

The checkered oilcloth conceals
the gaps, so I don't know where
to safely set my milk.
He brings the iron pot from the stove
and spoons out chili,
his pièce de résistance,
measuring it precisely,
sparingly.

Our mother smiles at us all,
and the room softens.

All day we'd played a thrilling game
of escape in the river. Icy water
knifed our legs, and the rocks
were slick and sharp as we trudged north,
but the guards spied us, so we rushed up the bank
to the railroad tracks and followed them for miles
and over a high trestle, I, groping my way along,
scared out of my mind at the gaping holes
below the crossties,
but the ladder held and led us

past the wilderness sun,
with the river following beside
and all the way back.

We try to, but we cannot eat his chili
for the heat. What should we do?
We look to her who loves us.

"Don, you put in too much hot sauce.
It burns their mouths."

He dumps our bowls back furiously
into his pot, and pours in sugar.
This fails, and then salt.

He throws it all out
and sulks from the room
back into his dread,
isolating presence.

Cold War Nerves

Mrs. Murza, our Orthodox babysitter from Lithuania, lived on the corner of Ninth and Livingston, and was what you'd call ample-bosomed. Clichés have their uses, and ample bosom was needed to quell the anxiety of a child growing up in the Cold War seeking the comfort of a grandmother figure, which is why I would walk to her house and soak up the strangeness of cabbage smells and her thick accent, thick like the slices of pumpernickel bread on her kitchen table where we'd sit and eat, talking like old friends. Her house was one of hundreds in Dominion Hills, all two-story brick built after the war with variations only in the shutters. Ours were green and belonged to Mr. Morse, the landlord, who had no idea of what went on in his house until the night he came for dinner and watched the puppet show my sisters and I put on for entertainment, with bickering so authentic our parents went white in the face, even whiter than they were, and that's another thing about Dominion Hills—it's where white flight landed from DC, and why, seeing the demographics, George Lincoln Rockwell and his storm troopers set up headquarters right across the highway in a farmhouse and went up to Crown Heights to open their terrifying trench coats and show their screaming twisted crosses to a crowd of Jews, so you can see why everyone was always on edge, but none more than my stepfather, who calmed himself each night with tequila and jazz because of all the secrets thumping inside his head, property of the CIA. I guess they owned us too because try as we might to escape (and my mother left three times), they always found us and returned us to our house on Ninth Street North. In sixth grade walking home from school with talk about the Cuban missile crisis ringing in my ears, and after I'd only just knelt behind Andrew Timotheou with my hands behind my head and the stench of his shoes in my face as we performed our drill, I knew the world was coming to an end. If it weren't for Mrs. Murza sharing bread with me under the peace of her sing-song blessing, I might have turned out wilder than I was starting to become, maybe doomed. Who knows what pull of grace abides in a person who escaped a homeland of millions murdered but never spoke of it, not even when I asked who the faded faces were in the photos on her mantel, just "Papa and Moder, and little girl is me!" Eventually, the era calmed down and the next genocide hadn't yet happened, but I searched out the story of Mrs. Murza's people and how their bodies were stacked in frozen camps and cattle cars in the name of war's clichés: "Blood and Honor," "Death or Freedom," "Peace to the World."

Onions

The ground is winter though the day is March.
In one hand seeds, in the other, a trowel,
because when your father is dying you're going to plant
onions in frozen dirt. Onions make sense in a time of coma.
Stab the dirt. Claw it. Stab and claw the cold riddle
begun in violence when you were small, that you papered over
hoping to hide from the others, fool them in motley layers of self.
No one could know what was down there below,
quivering, a naked snail. And he wasn't even your true father.
But keep digging, past every bitter loss, and maybe you'll find
it's really God under the sheets and your father, his heart crushed,
sleeps forgiven.

Weather of the House

I feel the weather of the house:

the mourning dove piping a dole in the eaves,
the ivy climbing on caterpillar feet and making a musty smell,
the plaster walls inside the house breathing a chalky air.

In the kitchen, a speck of a spider
keeps house in a corner web.
In the living room the couch sinks
from the heft of a man caught in the sun's haze
that veils the family pictures on the mantel.

There I am, hushing the children
so I can hear the house and what it knows
the way my mother learned air before a storm,
its exact weight, the better to fear.

But fear is not what dusts the attic floor,
the things in boxes I check on every few years:
twelve journals, the children's first clothes,
poems in my sister's hand that raise her face
to the bent light.

This is a known skin, felt all the hours
of my life as I reach or stoop or climb,
as I lie still on a summer night, alone
beside the man asleep, held instead
by much heat and the scripture of breath
I will recite in another house.

In this room in this house,
the weather wears like grief.

Blind Pink

I found it as if death had found me,
a rubbery fetus two girls from biology
had sneaked under my pillow.
Stink of pickling, the slickness
of that thick mute presence—to think
my sleep had spread over it all night
like a sow plastered with sun and grinning
at the wriggling under her magnificent slab.

Now, looking back, seeing the day thinning
and paling, I suppose the blind pink has always slept
with me, never moving at all, never
for all those nights being more
than unfulfillment, like colors dreamed
and spilled on the hard ground of morning.

Sister in a Coma

The fly couldn't hold
but buzzed and flailed
on my kitchen floor,
its wires throwing lost signals
the way a phone rings
unanswered in a room.
Its sensilla retained the dust of a grape
as you must surely feel the last sweet air
before reaching the point
where the brain unplugs its love
and looks sideways.

A Fall Too Far

When you stepped out for the ultimate shot
of the city's big shoulder,
was it for yet another thrill
to raise you farther from the pull of loves
you couldn't keep, just as you climbed
into your room the night your mother died,
the familiar U2 poster and the Edge
to see you through, and the photo
of her on your desk who gave you
your blue eyes and height
and never left St. Joseph's in your mind.
I think, darling nephew, her words
lived in you, all the way through your costly
slips, and through your broken loves
she held you, and from heaven
where every sparrow's fall is marked,
but how then could you fall so far?

"Photographer Eric Paul Janssen died tragically
on Monday afternoon at the age of 44.
While taking photos, he fell from the 20th floor
of the LondonHouse hotel in Chicago."
—DIYPhotography.net, October 18, 2017

Intercessor

I know why it was sent for me to see,
lying in its blood, a nameless bird
gutted by crows in the parking lot

speared by the murder hour by hour
as I watch from my window
aching anew in prayer

for my father, his vagrant mind.
Then out, I scatter the crows and dread
to stoop beside one

whose face the crows have left
unscathed, claiming only the heart,
not the flaccid legs, the slack neck,

those raveners standing by at arm's length
to guard their dead, their small fortune,
croaking at the woman in their way.

Summoned

(My mother told us a fable to explain menses to her three young daughters:
Every month, God cleans a room in our bodies to prepare for a baby who
will someday be planted there.)

Child, in a room cleared of dust
you are called before you are made.
You are clean and still as clay
from which breath is called to pain,
an unlit flame that burns the wind
or the star behind the quickening dark
as your unformed heart in its hollow waits
for the flutter of blood
when summoned.

You are loved before you are called
in your room of shadow and did not
want to go when the hand came
looking for the womb
where dust obscures your name
to sweep it for love, for change

while you hush in the unknown place
and yearn to be held this time
by the hand that made you
and bears your likeness,
with space between fingers
and light before dust burning
to take you as you are
and hold so hard it
hurts you.

Unbelievable

"He's crowning!"

Their green scrubs swarm
her open body like flies over meat,
but her mind refuses,
a little frozen box.

The only thing real
is the infinite second
after second, each a spiking
thorn, and screams raked
open from the kept
sea inside her flesh
as she pushes until her eyes bleed
and no child is coming, none
lives in her shabby womb

until he crowns, her son,
unbelievable
as Christ in his white
risen robe.

Royal Morning

(for Marcus)

The child wakes and reaches into pure day,
high-wired to test the lay of the crib
to make sure the sheet's firemen are climbing their ladders
and the monkey's glass eyes have kept their stare.
He tries the wooden bars for strength, shaking them sternly.
His legs bounce, happy as frogs,

and light spills ever brighter through the split blinds.
The ear turns cupward to the fields
where rooster and donkey trumpet the hour
and a pickup growls through gravel—oh glorious
day before mother wakes up
and the boy is prince of every prancing cloud.

A Bird's-Eye Birthday

(for Katy)

Did you hear the cardinal today, the first trill
after many tuneless months? You know,
he keeps a song under his royal red cloak
to pull out on your birthday with spring
on the wing. He spied your face,
pretty as the sun, showing up in the yard
with your boy who hops about like a rabbit,
and out of the king's heart flew *purty, purty, purty:*
three notes to count like cardinal numbers. He sang
to the light in your hair and to your hands dancing
on the run. He sang to the work you left on your desk,
along with bills (which oddly have no bills),
and to laundry unfolded and pots in the sink,
six books to read, a sorrow to soothe. He sang
to your smile and the Lord's smile shining
on the cows in the field behind the house
and on the chittering sparrows and distant coyotes,
but mostly he sang to your face shining in the eye
of your mate who loves you, a mate with strong good looks
(but not to his trophies, the deer mounts). He sang
to your mother and her red hair to which he is partial
and to the red squirrels fattened on corn, to the pair of cats
and their dog who warms them at night, to the stars nesting
in heaven he sang and sings of the seasons that were
and are to come, and of the happy day you were born,
carried by a breeze to the ground you stand on now,
and not a single feather to show for it.

The Light That Binds Us

Out of reach,
armed with your clothes and books in that bulging suitcase,
the air frozen when you stepped off the train into the dark
to heave and hoist the weight you brought from home.
It's midnight under the lamppost in Geneva and you,
not thinking but dreaming
with only that light and hardly a cent,
can't call.

It all ends well—
a ride to the hostel (the stranger was safe),
warmth and rest for cheap, Mont Blanc soon to astound—
miracle after miracle. I think the light follows you everywhere
despite the wolf in your mind when you were small that was a wolf,
the boy you thought was good who wasn't (and hungry, like a wolf),
the mirrors inside shattering the night you went missing.
Police at the door, questioning, brusque, too real,
too heavy a logic for my faint presence
to bear.

What else
can account for the harm you've outrun
each morning to now, to the lighter air
of a new country? There you are, alive,
my constant dreamer! And here I am,
saved again, breathless.

Nettie

She went out in forsythia,
a yellow day bursting over fields once
ablaze with corn and cotton, over the road
buried in asphalt that leveled it,
but it's still breathing underneath, pure dirt, hard
as a laborer's back, a road that follows
the earth's curve. The tall weeds walk
up and down, singing alongside, and I
was the girl walking with them,
telling stories to the wind.

Strange I wasn't sadder.
Grandma's laughter was always wanting out,
teased her mouth into a grin but had to hold itself in
for the worrisome times, and she could worry better
than anyone in Morgan County. Storms, the boys
running moonshine, Aunt Mattie going blind,
and my mother, the beauty among brothers
with fire in her mind.
That morning was the last time I breathed
the simple air. There's no one left
to pick the small, sweet jewels of time,
strawberries from her garden.

White Music at Dusk

An egret preens in a tree back-
lighted by the pendant sun slipping
to gild each strand

and you catch it on film:
the royal bird, the branch,
before the world goes dark.

We ride our bikes home
past the grave, blank sea,
past years when I never knew
how to picture my life.

But here the pine-strewn path in lowlight
returns the day's honey to my mind:
gold in the branches, the rinsed air,
the thought of you holding my face
as your brightest world.

Aubade

(after Dr. Williams)

Late Saturday morning
he drowses in the sun's syrup,
a lion-man heavy with dreams.

But even feeling his heat
I'm thinking about, well,
a frittata. I'll use the leftover
zucchini chunks and red onion
from last night

but that takes work and there's
a laundry list to check, so maybe
scrambled eggs are the answer,
with a dash of tarragon—

But on the other hand
(he's slipped it over my belly),
why fight the wanton hour?

I can always get some easy
plums out of the fridge
later.

Shelter Me Home

I.

Among the sea oats
I feel your gentleness,

feel it in the feathers of early light
that carry your face to me.

II.

How can your hands be so true,
planing the bark of renegade time,

hands that touch the hollows
and in reverence, ask nothing.

III.

Ahead of me, on the osprey trail—
your eye keen for the high trees
where nests are reborn every spring—

you have the stride of a boy,
the back of an alabaster king.

IV.

When you go down the ascending stair,
please cast your streaming cape my way
to shelter me going home.

Hungry Foxes

The things we leave on the table beside our favorite chairs
after the meal is done and the dishes put up:
my Lorca, your Howell, our scattered change—

The words we lose after the sun drops
and the crickets have drawn their bows,
after the rain moves in, the sad slow rain leaning toward the sea—

The feelings inside that shifted with the day, after the morning's
almost time, when your hand was new across my skin and we rose
like steam in the surging light that leads both toward

and away, a melting dream, a candle spending itself
in the noon of desire until the day bursts in a crimson bloom
and seagulls cry over the darkening waves,

and you with the fearless mind, the nesting arms
that held me through those several darksome deaths, O
love, where are we to be found? As sea grass hides

the hungry foxes, so night conceals
the faces of our change.

Cutting Hair

On the day to cut your hair
the sun has shaken
its shaggy mane of light
over the near ocean
over the trees behind our house
after a night of hunting
after birds have refilled the trees
and death has slipped
into the deep woods, its memory
scant as a snail's thread on the patio.

I wrap you in a cape and snug it with a clip.
How careful I must be, rounding
your good ear with scissors, the ear
my tongue loves to kiss, apricot-sweet,
and loves, too, the bad ear and its ghosts.
I thread your hair with a comb to gauge
length, silver in my loom.

I cut your hair in rhythm, remembering
the day you shaved what was left
of mine, how we walked
on a trail through the marsh, through
tufts of fog and I was slow as soup
of low tide, slow against your arm
remembering what it was like
not to lean, to be bright in my bones.

I see light differently now
painting the branches
behind our house, early, before

you're awake. It's more the gold
of afterlife, I think, a glimpse
before bodies take on all
that death.

Flying Yellow

Following then losing the leaf-gold trail
    I have no way to know if up will lead us out.
We see only downward and down is deep.
    I'm questioning my footfall and lean

against my stick. You've gone ahead
    to test the ground. This body,
not used to weakness, feels alone. It's a person
    in its own right, wanting to bless the mind

slipping on scree, to say, "Trust the light,"
    but the mind shuts its ears,
knows better than that foolish, stricken body
    and couldn't catch the flying yellow day if it tried.

II

Sister Sophia's Confession

Who would want young hands when old can heal
by feeling sorrow's Braille?—

the scarred hands of Nicholas, who carried a thief
from the burning camp at Klose,

and Claire, hands burled and bent,
who rubbed the scalps of untouchables,

and may I not forget Father Joachim's quaking
as he soothed the dying to bed.

These, my teachers, died to their desire.
Why should I wish for a girl's bland skin,

a page with no text, a mere flirting fan—slender fingers
stroking her lover's brow—

no, I never asked for such vain touch.
I loathe with all my heart that simpering flame.

Sister Sophia's Quarrel

What would I be if a poem born of my flesh
should escape, a fish-stinking clump
of words drawn from a vexed inward sea?

I'll never allow it. My rogue pen
might abhor rules, but I rule it
within the greater order.
Like the liturgy of the hours,
so must my words keep faith,
walk meekly within their lines,
be clean as cups on the shelf

      though Sister Ruth
seems always to miss the subtle tea stains
as she at prayer is also often missing.
She calls herself a poet, and knowing of my verse,
appeared last night at my cell, flush-faced, fluttering.

"Oh, Sister! Permit me to read these lines.
They came to me unbidden, and in a white heat.
Forgive my great impudence, but see how I tremble
to tell you the Spirit said the poem is for *you*."

(Imagine the crumb telling the loaf how to be bread!)

She pressed on with her shocking verse:

"Better honey from the rock than the rock.
Better to sin (bless his wounds) than be safe.
Think of the one who spurned men's commands
and let a whore perfume and adore him
with passionate hair, who stretched out his hand

to bloom a stump—on a Sabbath, at that,
and in the presence of clergy."

And then, she hurried out, but not before leaving
with words that worried me all night
like a mouse gnawing inside a wall:
"It's true, Sister Sophia. Art is strict
as the honeycomb. But wild
as love, the ecstatic honey."

Mary Rowlandson's Removes

"When others are sleeping, mine eyes are weeping."

In the beginning she was called often
to relate scenes of blood and flame
from the Tenth of February,
with the goodwives crying to hear her tell
of her dead child turned under barren dirt
and left alone on a hill as she was led away—
and how she marked with scripture each remove:
the camp of snow and fever, the swamp of sinking,
the ground where Praying Tom dangled white fingers,
the begging from fire to fire for any niche against
the frozen black void she read as inscrutable love,
for her mind, forged on Calvin, would not bend

though sometimes, in the starved light before day
she would hear the child pleading for water,
pleading from just over the ridge,
and she would cry out, her wits unlashed
as stars withdrew their nets,
but her legs failed her, snared by sleep.
(What mercy, she would later say,
to quell her madcap flight and savage fate.)

This telling of her inmost trial she came to fix in print,
could hardly believe it was she herself there in the tent
slabbering over a horse's foot snatched from a child
or swearing in the face of pagan taunts—how is it
she secretly craves that state even now as others sleep,
a manic flame to burn the ordered words,
the syntax that gives shape to every scream.

Dorothy Bradford: "A Very Grown Sea"

Cradling my hand, cuffed in a ruffle,
he asked, would I cross the sea?

Candlelight spilled on the table,
lighting the plate of bones.

How could I know my own mind,
swayed by his hollow cheeks
and grave, bent shoulders?

Just as I never told
my love for patterned prayers
and painted glass that kept me safe
in the straits of a rote God who took no thought
for the brightly errant threads of a dreamer,

neither could I confess I had no faith
for the trip, would rather brave
the known foes of Leyden
than a gaping beyond.

For I have striven to live by Sarah's rule,
saying "Yes, I will follow after,"
binding my streaming hair in the bonnet,
shunning my prayer book hid in satin folds,

yielding my flesh to him but never voicing at all
the cries of buried tides for fear he'd think me
wanton like Strangers ever seeking
to draw us in, how I faltered at his throbbing hands

as I am faltering here in this hole
with the lantern swinging
and mothers and children doubled over,

the mountainous sea pitching us like a ball.
"Pukestocking," the sailors call us
and leer like devils. Oh,

I know they can see clear down
the well of my soul where I have kept
from him, even him, a dread
that gives way to strangely
painted thoughts not meet for one elect.

Often, I visit a lush banquet and taste,
but all is emptied, wasted in these waves

where I wish more than life
to fling my gray stocking
and lie in a dreamless hollow.

Two Boston Ladies Visit Phillis Wheatley on Her Deathbed: 1784

Here, Mistress Sewell,
take my arm and come close.
See how low she lies,
beyond reach of fame or friend.
Oh, never mind the mice.
Let us honor pure genius.

It's she who acclaimed our town
with her vaulted rhymes, and bannered the great names—
she, the sable darling, the church's pride

and yet,
        looking across oceans,
knowing the contradictions,
she wrote other poems . . .

Yes, contradictions! As a slave
she soared on her charmed quill,
petted by the mistress who immersed her in books,
praised by a countess and the good Mr. Franklin.
Yet in freedom, she was slave to floors and chamber pots.

        And where, you ask, might her husband be?
He who wore the lace cravat and owned fine books
sinks in a debtors' jail, perhaps too clever
in the eyes of our race, he is.

No, she can't hear us. Alone, apart, African in soul,
she dreams, I think, of a land not cold as this.

Strangled Roses: A Portrait

*(Edgar Allan Poe's mother, Eliza, and his wife, Virginia Clemm Poe, both died of
tuberculosis and at the same young age of twenty-four. At Virginia's death and upon the
realization he had no image of her, Edgar commissioned an artist to paint her corpse.)*

"How grace does guide your hand, Mr. Frye—
To limn her back to life, the chestnut hair,
the sacred lily whiteness."

* * *

His voice flaps in the lamp-dark,
a moth roused from a fold of brocade.

Has he no heart for the dead, for me,
Sissy, whose chin he has horribly let sink,

when in time he always tilted it
to set my eyes on even plane with his,

stooping at bedside to read *my* poem
as if to loosen me from iron breath:
"Love will heal these weakened lungs . . ."
But the verses failed in mid-air,
too faint for the brazen dark.

He wiped my scarlet mouth,
pleading as if he were the child
who once buried curls
in his mother's sodden breast.

Tonight I fear he is not Eddy,
pacing like a beast, his rough hands
draping my shoulders in a marble pose,
bloodstains in the sheets like strangled roses.

God, do not let him stroke me to half-life,
the flat crepuscular light a mask on my face,
gravid eyeballs aching under lids,
fingers that once brushed his noble cheek
now wrested into my lap.

He means to keep me safe in the gilt frame,
to encrypt the undersound of heaving lungs:
his mother wrack'd in a maze
of blackened blood he cannot flee,
the smothering candle-smoke wavering
like his own vaporous small shadow.

* * *

"Make haste, Mr. Frye, before dawn breaks—
Seal the lowered gaze, the ivory neck—
Embalm with paint her beauty,
let her frozen mouth ring for joy!"

Raggedy Ann on God

Oh god who art a pushover,
loves rubber babies or any
claysoft, titadoring thing:
Why have you forsaken me?
Is it my arrowbones?
The scars I see with?

Go on, daddy, try me.
Stick your sun like a gun in my ribs—
it's flesh you smell, not wax,
and believe me, mister,
these wings are prayers,
not pasteboard.

I will claw your dimpled hands
and rake your eyes and
twist that plushy image
like a dove's neck.
I will not have you amused
and babbling with your Play-Doh:

I'm shaped too like a cross
to let you off so easy.

Adam by the Sea

Water hasn't blushed this way,
felt its shore so rosily stroked
nor known such private light
since the first dawn
when Adam by the sea
was watching the sunrise
and feeling out of place in his body,
his strength trapped in muscles,
his desire walled inside skin.
He had no name for the sting
of salt, the sting of being made
for what was not yet made,
not joined in a rush of flesh,
the ruddy thrust unnamed
and ripe with death.

Someone Who Was Expected

"I do not feel that I am the product of chance, a speck of dust in the universe,
but someone who was expected, prepared, prefigured. . . ." —*Jean-Paul Sartre*

I was there
        when a boy saw his shadow for the first time
spilling out of himself like another boy.
        He waved to his mother—
"It's me, it's me!"
        and danced from boy to boy
                on the moon-white lawn.

Blind Sartre too saw himself for the first time.
        A hand—was it a shadow of his own? Or
was *his* the shadow, the allegory? —
        that hand descending, and death in the room waiting
            with the patience of Job.

He felt his useless eyes waken, scan the room
        for his friend, old rebel turned Jew, who'd been keeping watch
but was out for a smoke when the hand swept in like a force
        to show the exit: self-knowledge, pure being beloved,
        and Sartre, lucid to the end, knew it was so.

        The air surged with sense, incense.

Because You Are Cherished

(In memory of poet and writer Eve Shelnutt, 1941–2015)

It was rain, the rain calling,
not your nightgown heavy with night
not the blur of your body leaving its work
nor the tortured rocks of your words,
your hoarse, garbled goodbyes
that broke at the last like geodes.
I carry their light with me

and wonder that the spines of your books
stay stiff despite the chaos and drift inside,
the funny, tragic people that look like us
and "leave a place for us, even the dead,"
you wrote. How bravely you stiffened,
how long against death. And then
it was time to lay down thought,
let the rain come lightly.

Learning Curve

He arrives on time for me to okay
his research plan, and I listen,
observing the bones
of his face—how private,
how strained his skin—
and eye the neat notebook tabs
demarking his subjects, a defiance,
I suspect, against the mayhem
in his marrow.

I consider
how his blood must have churned
when he read his first essay aloud
the week before, standing there
in front, frayed, a little shaky,
speaking words like everyone else
but with his steel
frailty delivering to us the gift
of his costly knowledge.

"Approved!"
and then he rises
from his chair
like a king.

The Test

After hours of study and stress she falls
asleep dreaming of Thomas and a picnic.
The sun's hand warms her cheeks,
the sky sings its blue song.
Kids are splashing in the creek
and she finds the tree with big arms
and shade to eat sandwiches under,
to laugh over words that rhyme with orange,
feeling his eyes on her face go quiet
because he sees her differently,
the dark river of her hair, her kaleidoscope mind.
Doubt fades in his reaching look.

But she wakes to rain.
The dash to the car is drenching
and the room's already full.
She finds a desk in the back and feels
her insides clench with an old fear
that freezes the puzzles on the page
everyone else is solving, and,
as they turn in their tests one by one,
she hears them thinking, "Not smart enough."

But didn't Thomas say, "*Look,
you think in colors, you dance your words*"?
She zips her raincoat, turns nothing in
and shakes as she goes out the door
because of what she knows she can't be
and the aborning idea of who she really might be.

Postscript, from Carolyn

and I have swallowed pills,
drawn the bath,
bolted the door.

The dog, my drop-eared darling,
whines downstairs.

I slip out of my motley.
Poor sad heap—someone else
will gather you.

Clarity chills my brain. They'll find
the ribbon of blood from my nose
but no other show. Not

the Holy Ghost
with his white
porcelain shoulder
cradling my head.

She Dreams of Snow and Morning

How to rise from this heavy
snow, the floor
spread out like a waste,
the bone-white cup beyond reach.

How to seize that near light
of sippable warmth,
the cognac-sweet enticement.

Let my mind burn with it,
my tongue catch fire
that makes holy.

Let the life I took from myself
come back in joy or pain

Only please wake me up.

Kite Surfer

What will he do now in bigger wind,
bigger than the dragon flame that zapped
his friend across the sands, collapsing the world
in the millionth war, burnt men shambling
in the orange flare—he steers his kite
across the sea doing hoochie glides, knowing
the lure of muscle, the taunt that corners blind forces,
the power of his control bar. He's lost sight of land,
lost guilt in his death slide, the wind lofting him
high above the graves of the drowned.
He rises like memory canceling itself, freeing itself
for the purity of height, his canopy its own small sky
to hoist him heavenward, away from his brain
that knows and keeps count of every costly flinch
(his M-16 stalled when his fingers shook like girls').
No heartbreak here. The wind is all for now.

Flashbacks

One by one they take their seats before the young,
spreading out snapshots of the smooth-jawed khaki boys
they were back then, with the Browning automatic
slung over a shoulder, or in sailor suits
piled around their Bofors guns, grinning.
Some bring souvenirs—a red Japanese flag, a leaflet
dropped over Korea, the yearbook of a ship that later sank
with all its fresh-faced crew.

They've lived their second, ever-settling lives
for a long time and move about the ordinary fixtures of the world
on unsteady legs, but now and then they see a flash of faces
never coming home—the reason for the interviews
being to dredge the sea or comb the fields for glimpses

as if the young could understand that wars must be
and men must die, or grasp that Myers or Clark,
mere kids like these, cocky, the best of pals,
would wind up choking under flaming beams
or writhing legless on a frozen hill—

when just the night before they'd mocked
and horse-played, sucked on cigarettes, bragged of girls—
What words can match such weight: the heavy, daily sound
of bodies sliding off gurneys into the churning waves,
the stink of ovens stuffed with the starved.
One by one they try their best to tell it
to kids whose faces mirror what they were.

Buchenwald

I nearly bought that shirt
spun of fine cotton
and tailored to my exact fit.
The treasures you find in thrift stores!

Crammed in with hundreds,
its sheen stood out
in the shabby rack,
but when I looked closer

there it was, a yellow stain
where my heart would be.
I hung it back and left,
Jack Lorber on my mind

as I drove by neat neighborhoods
in the rain, house after brick house
with invisible people going about
their lives as we all do.

He was one of the soldiers
who liberated Buchenwald
in nearby Weimar where neighbors
denied the acrid stench

and went on as usual—until
furious General Patton forced
them to march five miles up
and back down Ettersberg Hill

carrying the open-eyed bodies of bone
to heave into pits. I saw the pictures:
a woman in pumps and Sunday dress
shielding her eyes from the stacks,
the rest of us crying, gasping, looking away.

The Light Left On

Irene and her story—one,
no more than two Polish stories she ever told me.
Her voice was brittle, and her hands worried so
to let nothing slip from place in her tidy rooms
high over Georgetown.

We drank sherry in late September,
and when she found my trust
she named her lost, most especially
Uncle mustached Mort who'd brought her gifts
from his shop, little tin windup toys—a clown
with clapping cymbals, a horse-drawn
milk wagon. And Dorothy, her mother's best friend
smiling grandly in the picture, the baby in her arms
adoring the face aglow.

Then to work, why I'd come, to go through her poems,
the collection she called "The Light Left On."
It never saw print, though Lord knows, I tried.
What friendship came from all those rejections,
what hopes we revived time and again.

Priest in the Treatment Room

(for Father Nigel Mumford)

Drowsed with potions, we had our fun
as the shrill signals waned and we slipped
deeper into our plush recliners, glad to be sleeping
with disease at bay, to have thoughts teased from us drip
by drip, the faces of son or sister dim despite
the huge, over-bright room that out of nowhere
welcomed a priest riding in a scooter, a black-clad Jesus,
but one laboring to breathe as he landed at someone's chair
and blessed her bags hung from hooks, three bags of poison,
blessed a head bent and scared against his hand, but oh,
you knew he knew what it's like to be pitted against those stakes
with all of us hoping on the skids.

III

III

There Is the Lake and There Is the Street

We left the street for the timeless green
lens of water. The only signposts
were cypress trees with fluted dresses
who danced when our heads were turned,
the way trees in love dance everywhere,
who led us to longer and farther
reaches of silence, past the turtle's head,
the egret's curve, our paddles resting
across our laps as villages of knobs
drifted by on their way to the sun's
slow commerce. Past the water striders'
elegant script and our need for words,
for memory. We held it the whole afternoon,
that enchanted face, then let it slip into the water.

Light, Hard-Earned

(for Stephen)

Light, hard-earned, is sweet:
jasmine perfuming an island
come back from a storm.

It coaxes with aplomb
like a stray dog drawn
from the weeds to a whistle.

It's air as small as a jar
in a cave-in,
life enough for one.

It pinkens a son born blue
to the freshness of lotus.
The mother kisses him with tears.

Who can understand
how, at the drained hour,
light may visit the crushed
or condemned, light so sure

it stops the heart
and brings the world
to its new morning

the starfish to the tide.

The High, Hunted Trees

(At the Constance du Pont Darden Preserve
in Virginia, the endangered red-cockaded woodpecker
nests only in mature, fire-resistant pines.)

This quiet grows from our not seeing
the bird we came to see
in the pine grove forged by fire,
in the hollow of her heartwood,

the quiet of a chapel empty
but for the sun that fills it
and names each tree "my lightfall,"
"my greenlit singer," and lingers

as we pause on the pathway
to scout the high trees
for the telltale sign, a red cockade,
the little resistance badge he wears

like one of God's revolutionaries,
ill-matched against encroachers
of silent spaces, but spared
by one who asked why we kill

the gift for gain, and bought
the woods. Leaving, we take
a last look at the pines climbing
the lordly shafts of sun.

Marsh Marigolds

Brown edges on all
but the marsh marigold
unbuttoned like a bride.

Pure yellow! Spring in fall!

My walk takes me far from old despair,
his spittled beard and suffocating arms.

I've left his park bench and sour shirt for the slow
tides, his raw ankles for the free-gliding fish.

Late sun releases dragonflies.

Sea Frolic

"Now is the time of grace." —*Menno Simons*

The sea, the frocks, the neat white caps staying put
      in all that froth—To come across such girls!

They leap among crashing hills, three bodies lithe
      in clinging flowers, and beyond the swell,

dolphins wheel in time to tell the endless gleam—
      Why Father on shore is smiling in his beard,

his flock released in the aqua curve to fly
      in summer dresses.

Leitmotif

Leaf aloft, leaf spirit:
   bird notes thread the trees with the gold-tinted
breeze taking off to set the woods aflame
   while the swamp lies sleeping in cypress dark,
the knobs like gnomes assembled to keep the spell
   so none can wake the frogs and set them glugging.
Down to the mudflats crawling with mud crabs
   and fiddlers waving their same languid claws for eons
as it was in Grendel's day, coming up out of the fen.
   Borne by the tide to range the sea plains, pelicans skim
the breaking swells; the sky bends low in a silver streaming
   reach to the edge where the last leaf floats and falters.

The Weight of Less Light

Summer's late blooms sink in sunlight
as if a hand were herding us through time,
down to the cricket, wee clock in the grass

to the water snake sleek among rocks
tuned to the tide and the rush of fish
in brackish brown and soon called away

to the toothless man on a bench
and his bearded friend, both old
grown older and tired from weather

down to the squirrel and her frenzied hunt,
to the grasshopper dragging itself in the dirt,
to the last blackbird flown from the marsh,

a red smear of wings, a cry to pierce the heart.
Down to the moon, that white drum above us
drumming our blood and the seasons inside.

Already the sea oats bend low, pressed down
by the weight of less light and the shadow
of a great invisible.

Dark Current

Once launched
the water moves by strange
power, keeps a steady pace
as it strings the sky along.
White flocks graze
on innocent blue.

It carries the trees and a boy's tossed twig,
streams past osprey nests now emptied
and travels all the way to sea
where the dead don't stay long,
renounced by a fecund anarchy
and rolled to shore, fetid and gleaming

like a whale I saw, a juvenile humpback
jarred from course by naval sonar
and slashed by a propeller,
the stillborn entrails loosed from the wound.
Its fins were studded with barnacles,
its black majesty striped white.

I took in the fog planet of its eye,
the impossible girth of silence
that once was song. The waves
kept thrashing the world where I stood
as if rage could ever thwart the force
aborting and aborting.

Gray Distances

The loneliness of their long whistles
the sound full of their whiteness,
even in community they are lonely,
miles of loneliness across the rain-
beaten water as they have come to overwinter,
to fly the gray distances from there to here,
to be the wings of longing, to plumb
the sky and sea, landing and leaving
like arrows from the bow of God,
the air crying for love of swans.

Peacock Lost in Tornado

When the great wind
took aim at the Harper's farm,
it swallowed only Peabody.

The barn was damaged,
implements twisted,
but not a hair on a head
was lost, only
Peabody's feathers.

Later that day, a rainbow.

Out of Place

The dark was darker than back East,
steeped in trees and stone, not thin as nights
blown off the ocean. This dark
swallowed even the road I strained to see.
The headlights did what they could
to map the unknown but didn't spot
the coyote in time, only his partner
in the other lane who made it
back to the woods. The car broke
where it struck. The creature's remains
knocked all the way to the light
left on at home.

Great Crested Flycatchers

Patience, I need a hand.
The ground's harder today
than yesterday.
It's a long wait to catch
the flycatchers
dipping in and out of the hollow
to feed their young.
My bones ache,
but I'm holding for a poem,
a pure whistle,
the hillock of their head
and quick yellow.
Across the lake, young ospreys cry
from their nests in the high snags,
bring us wings.

Warlord

"No wonder the Aztecs believed warriors cut down in battle would be reincarnated as hummingbirds—ounce for ounce, there's probably no fiercer creature on Earth." —Jason Bittel

Creature scarcely bumblebee size
launches from God's own finger.
Fierce among flowers, he's a Samurai
fending off rivals brazen to venture near
his private nectar sipped from bee balm's
lips, those scarlet beauties shielded by mighty
wingbeats driven by his furious heart.

Poseur

It's the orchid bee's lucky day.
There in the shallow fen his bride awaits,
perfumed and posh in pink, her velvet lips
quivering, and all for him, a love so true
he lands at once but weds in vain
the double-dealing bee orchid posing
for his pollen, which he loses,
like a fool his money.

I Feed Them Anyway

They're soldier-like,
prowling for food in gray jackets.
Weather beats them down
but they take on rain
and cold anyway,
starving and fighting to eat,
split-eared, tail-bitten.

When I was a child,
the cold went into my hands
feeling their hard fur.
My uncles shot squirrels for fun
and I prayed they'd come back
to the world I knew,
though it too was torn
from things you'd think
shouldn't touch a child.

I've tamed them
from the woods
to eat from my hand
and confess the indulgence,
my protest of nature's ban
against the dark, bright eyes
that let me in.

Sea Urchin

On the counter
a drop of blood
from one that had suffered
under God's eye,
a curio, fragile as blown glass,
plucked from the shore
on a glittering day

but now, purpled to dark
of thorns I hadn't known
were shivering spines.

Deadly Game

The zoo hippo died of pennies,
lipsticks, a camera.
His tongue, a huge pink slab,
closed on everything thrown.
His polka dot eyes
watched the whole time,
blinking and watching, helpless
to stop the fun.

I stood between my parents near the rail,
popcorn in hand, hoping for a toss.
People in loud shirts kept pushing toward
the purple-gray clown in his pool.
They swallowed me, I never got a turn.

When I read that he died,
I thought of his mouth, a cave
he couldn't hide in,
and his tongue, naked and blind.

Cicadas

Who can break the spell of cicadas?
   Chained to time, they chant in step all night,
      starting and stopping on a dime. If

you happen to wake from a dream where you were sucking
   on sweet disorder, say, the juice of a geode
      squeezed from the daily rubble, or milk from the moon—

if you ascend from the snugness and there,
   to crush your hope of singing in trees,
      the violent, the black unbroken hauls you in,

don't think you'll escape with your life.
   What pulls you out you'll never find down here.

Tufts of Him Drift Down

No longer the sandscape where I named the shells
and the shorebirds rounding the waves, praised the daily skies
unfurling coral sunbursts or gray solemnity, but always
a heaven in view—

Here, the yard is mostly moss, old time, old oaks.
I had a hunger for stars one night and lay on my back
for a glimpse, but the dark was tangled up in branches
and Quentin returned to my thoughts as he has of late, at night.

There's an hourless space before waking, a womb or urn
safe from hope's cruel feathers, an escape from hawkish time
that seizes what it likes from the sky and rips apart a future.
Tufts of him drift down.

So, where does this leave me now? You don't say.
Cicadas drown Your voice, or maybe it's my own heart
clanging in chains. The stars know. They sing in voices
far and pure. Unlike time bleeding into morning.

Memento Mori

In the kitchen corner
a speck drew me to its web.
Obsessed, I watched it move
like music across its line.

This wearied me, my mania.
I studied the mote several times a day
and sometimes blew on the web
to make sure it danced.

Then, it didn't.

It hung there for a week
until I thought to sweep it away,
sadly relieved of my little death.

Robins

Tame, almost, and common
as clay, the robins bestrew
our lawns and whistle in sycamores
well beyond dusk.
Unfazed by revving cars or raucous
crows, they sing to the third heaven
where better ears than ours
applaud their arias.
Before dawn, the bards fish
in dew-starred earth, hatched red
from the early sun
but with night on their wings.
Seen like this, how rare the robins.

Writing Poems with Ghost Crabs

They freeze by their holes
for many maddening minutes,
obsessive, holding time itself
in ghostly pincers,
as words themselves will stall
and fix on nothing.
The fear is that the nothing will go on.

But maybe their stalk-eyed stare
is toward a different air,
a nod, a nudge that breaks
the spell to send them dashing
down their hollows to dish out sand
and toss it lightning-quick at the world
to build a shore.

Visitor

The deer arrives, wasting, and missing
half an antler. He nuzzles the leaves unwarily
for the broken pumpkin and lies down,
the same gray of earth, beside my fence.

IV

The Entry

(The Gospel of Luke 19:28–40)

Plush in Mary's guarded womb
with scent of heaven recent in his brain,
he rocked along the rough-hewn road to birth.

But Mary felt it all, the jolt of every up-
and downward mile by the Jordan's forest,
hills and flatlands, threat of thieves and lions.

She so young to bear the weight,
fullness of the God-child wanting out—
Oh, but he *would* out and ride again, though not

on that threadbare road. This road's laden
with cloaks and fronds. Clamor of songs
and shouts disrupt the air, but the donkey

bears her load without complaint
and all of it heavy: She hears that other strain
in the fugue of hosannas, the Devil's Interval

no one else can hear except perhaps
the innocent one on her back laboring
toward a hill, a skull on this day of adoration.

The Betrayal

From the beginning he loved the man,
though his nature was kin to the goat,
and said, "Come, I've saved a place for you,"
and there, smiling at his friend beside,
he blessed the wine, the bread, the bitter herbs
and all the men reclining.
The friend leaned in, as if moved like the rest
at the Master's weighted words spoken over his last
Pesach, feast of his body and blood in perpetuity
"until I drink with you again in my Father's kingdom."
Then with a knowing hand Jesus fed his friend
the dripping sop, sorrow of garum, the fish sauce.

Passion

"Eli, Eli, lema sabachthani?"

Won't somebody feed me,
find me in the dark:
my head, stone-heavy on my chest,
my bones brittle as winter.

In my dreams I always see the kingdom of God.
In my heart I hear the white peals summoning past
all pity, past the bruised brow where sadness never sleeps
and the hunted creature slips into thorny nightfall.

In my dreams, in my long-ago life you strode with me
over the high hills, free as the capering goats
and with me down into quarantined towns
where a single word was enough to break the bars

of incurables and thieves. I thought so then, but now
my tongue has swelled to woolen thickness and my skin
is ablaze from a thousand stings and I confess, with tears,
I don't believe the light.

Resurrection Fruit

I caught the fruit before they pinned me in harlequin time,
and ate it whole: a small, ripe sun, a joy inside my ribs
when the pitch-black storm riddled my heart
and made a riddle of souls I sheltered there.

But even as I rose and sank on the bleeding tree,
as the wind shrieked denials to my fraying will
and the howling hills drew close to savage their spoil,
I felt a current escorting me up from the fret of flesh,

the faces of scorn and desire, from the wrecked
earth full of bones I know will live, O Glory!
How strong the ladder of Your arms to raise me
shivering, newborn, into jubilation bursting forever.

Goldberg Variations on Summer Peaches

Peeling peaches at the sink, smitten
by five suns bleeding at the center,
listening to Bach as the golden
rapturous juice throbs like music
in a robin's throat.

With dripping wrists I wave away
a fly drawn to the sweet spillage
and taste every ruby note,
Jesus kissing me.

Something She Heard about You

Hearing you like to conceal yourself
she looks for you in slight gestures and lowly glances,
the man with stumbling words, the girl with shaved head.

There you are in a broken loaf, a sliding tear.
You in the plum-sweet gaze, the offered chair.

She says it's changed her life, the glory of the hidden,
hand not telling hand, cries making no sound,
ashes acknowledged, goods left unclaimed.

She will go to her grave emptied as a borrowed sack
but her soul—fat with secrets, ripe as a pupa—
will open at first kiss like a universe.

Keeping the Bowl

I want to tell You why I'm keeping the bowl,
why of all the things I'm giving away—
things crazed, gouged, scorched, no longer useful—
I've chosen to save this, my mother's bowl
with faded cherry border, fruit of her mind
as it was when she lay shrunken as a child,
the lamb of her cheek and shorn head newly made
in the kindness of last light.

How perfectly You must see that the past holds far
too great a claim on me, the boxes of grief—
so many houses! Each move leading to
the final emptying where nothing arrives
but the trembling, homeless soul
asking for preservation, asking
to be loved, the shamefully
marred hands cupped for a token,
even a small remembrance of the hollow
You of all beings might wish to fill.

Risen

Rain loosed through willows wakes the sleepers.
Their lead eyes open to newborn light.
Their hair, lately kissed, grows in the grave
that still brings tears on earth but elsewhere
flames into white filigree, like threads of stars,
and the ashes of their hands
        sing like lutes.

Traveling Light

I caught the gleam of her silver bracelet
as she stroked her son's back in church
that Sunday the missionary came.
The gesture invited a burst of sunlight
that poured through the stained glass
and over our shoulders, down the aisles,
swam through our ribs to reach the world's night side.

Imagine the miracle. Loving her son that instant
changes the plight of the ninth child
in the *kibanda matope,* the one the missionary
said was born blind and given the most meager
share of meal in preference to others
who needed more to live, but he comes to see
after all because someone was sent,
and the light is always looking.

("Kibanda matope" is Swahili for mud hut.)

Shirley's Spaniel

To be a priest
is to widen your arms

to hold the great sorrow,
the stillborn hour

the hour night fell
like a drunk along the canal

slipping into the black mouth
of oblivion, and you laid your head

on your arms to rest forever
but being a priest

you have to wake them up
those arms, and make them take heart

for the ache of holding up a world
small and trembling, full of fever

or bone-thin and silent as snow.
Sometimes you hold so long

you become the other.
Is it so, is it possible?

Shirley's spaniel took on her seizures
but one day missed the step

and lost the field. The priest said
it happens that love can grow so large

no life can hold it. First it seeps, then flows
then floods and someone walks out

and someone disappears.

Aunt Helen's Hand

Skin has a sweetness, even papery
vine-veined hands cold to touch.
When I hold Aunt Helen's hand
to my cheek, I can believe
it's fruiting elsewhere,
that the purple bruises from needles
and the rawness of her radiated flesh
will bloom in another light.

Sometimes, looking at my own veins
so prominent and blue now, veins like hers
that ached from needle jabs, skin that burned
under the beam—and when I think
of everyone like me, maimed and pulled away
by time, I dream of hands that hold us fast,
reaching through flame and frost for us,
the beautiful fruit of his wounds.

A Bidding Prayer

for all the lost eyes and limbs
wandering over there: the severed
head that made Herodias smile

and each head that darkly soaks the dust
but once nestled near a mother's heart,
her luscious breasts promising
lasting, improbable love.

For Robert Hanna's leg ripped with grapeshot
and his clumsy government-issue stand-in.
For soldiers like him blasted and sawn,
their parts misplaced in foreign lands.

For minds that never stop being killed.

For Van Gogh's ear and his lost sanity
spilling into zinnias. For poets charged
with words and hung for words.

For the honeycomb child
dismembered from her dream,
and what of her golden, peddled parts?

For Grandfather's index finger
tapping a tune over there.
For my missing breast, so lately fondled.

Over there, in the country of heaven,
the Body most broken, most whole
carries the sad, unbearable bones
until they're all gathered home.

More Lavish than Wisteria

Because you send apples to dance at my feet
and wisteria wild in the trees
to toss passionate jewels:
the purple and the glittering green
that awakens praise in my heart,
a wick too small for such gifts
of sky-sprung songs, a thousand
tunes in the poplars, how can I love you back
who fills my belly full of bread, who sent the man
to be lamb-sweet across my skin
and the sun's candle to waken words
that rise out of sleep's gray river:
to be warmed by the mist that one day
will lift me high and away,
how to say thanks, mere wind-fleck, me.
It's all I know to say to you who set me on this
spinning blue now, nudging me to let you deeper in,
blood of my blood, breath of desire.

ACKNOWLEDGMENTS

For his invaluable advice along the way, I wish to thank my long-time friend Larry Richman. For his encouragement, insights and loving support over the years of the book's making, I'm grateful to my husband, Wayne Rhodes. For being my first and most enthusiastic audience, I thank my sister, Leslie, and also my children, Katy, Stephen, and Emily for being all ears when I read my poems to them. For belief in my work, I'm indebted to my former editor, Mark Burrows, and for carefully tending these pages into print, I'm thankful to Robert Edmonson and Paraclete Press.

Grateful acknowledgment is made to the editors of the following journals where the poems in this collection first appeared, sometimes in slightly altered form:

Aethlon: Journal of Sport Literature, "Kite Surfer" (reprinted in Sport Literature Association's special teaching issue)

Alaska Quarterly Review: "Blind Pink"

Anglican Theological Review: "Mary Rowlandson's Removes" and "Flying Yellow"

Appalachian Journal: "Goldberg Variations on Summer Peaches"

ARTS: The Arts in Religious and Theological Studies: "A Bidding Prayer"

Atlanta Review: "Tufts of Him Drift Down"

The Christian Century: "Gray Distances," "A Theme Perhaps for the Plague," and "Traveling Light"

Edgar Allan Poe Review: "Strangled Roses: A Portrait"

Image: "Cutting Hair" and "Shirley's Spaniel"

Midwest Quarterly: "There Is the Lake and There Is the Street"

Mothers Always Write: "Royal Morning"

Penwood Review: "Risen"

Poetry East: "Shelter Me Home" and "White Music at Dusk"

St. Katherine Review: "Intercessor," "Sister Sophia's Confession," and "Unbelievable"

Slant: "Aubade"

Sow's Ear Poetry Review: "Flashbacks" and "Sea Urchin"

Spiritus: "The High, Hunted Trees" and "Passion"

Spoon River Poetry Review: "Dorothy Bradford: A Very Grown Sea"

The Cresset: "Something She Heard About You"

The Windhover: "More Lavish than Wisteria"

Town Creek Poetry: "Dark Current"

Several of the poems also appeared previously in chapbooks:

Weather of the House (Sow's Ear Press, 1994) and *Hungry Foxes* (Aldrich Press, 2013)

"The Entry," "The Betrayal," "Passion," and "Resurrection Fruit" were exhibited during Holy Week, 2020, in a collaboration with Spectra visual artists at Fellowship Bible Church in Rogers and Fayetteville, Arkansas, and then virtually on social media during the coronavirus pandemic.

ABOUT PARACLETE PRESS

Who We Are

As the publishing arm of the Community of Jesus, Paraclete Press presents a full expression of Christian belief and practice—from Catholic to Evangelical, from Protestant to Orthodox, reflecting the ecumenical charism of the Community and its dedication to sacred music, the fine arts, and the written word. We publish books, recordings, sheet music, and video/DVDs that nourish the vibrant life of the church and its people.

What We Are Doing

BOOKS | PARACLETE PRESS BOOKS show the richness and depth of what it means to be Christian. While Benedictine spirituality is at the heart of who we are and all that we do, our books reflect the Christian experience across many cultures, time periods, and houses of worship.

We have many series, including *Paraclete Essentials*; *Paraclete Fiction*; *Paraclete Poetry*; *Paraclete Giants*; and for children and adults, *All God's Creatures*, books about animals and faith; and *San Damiano Books*, focusing on Franciscan spirituality. Others include *Voices from the Monastery* (men and women monastics writing about living a spiritual life today), *Active Prayer*, and new for young readers: *The Pope's Cat*. We also specialize in gift books for children on the occasions of Baptism and First Communion, as well as other important times in a child's life, and books that bring creativity and liveliness to any adult spiritual life.

The MOUNT TABOR BOOKS series focuses on the arts and literature as well as liturgical worship and spirituality; it was created in conjunction with the Mount Tabor Ecumenical Centre for Art and Spirituality in Barga, Italy.

MUSIC | PARACLETE PRESS DISTRIBUTES RECORDINGS of the internationally acclaimed choir *Gloriæ Dei Cantores*, the *Gloriæ Dei Cantores Schola*, and the other instrumental artists of the *Arts Empowering Life Foundation*.

PARACLETE PRESS IS THE EXCLUSIVE NORTH AMERICAN DISTRIBUTOR for the Gregorian chant recordings from St. Peter's Abbey in Solesmes, France. Paraclete also carries all of the Solesmes chant publications for Mass and the Divine Office, as well as their academic research publications.

In addition, PARACLETE PRESS SHEET MUSIC publishes the work of today's finest composers of sacred choral music, annually reviewing over 1,000 works and releasing between 40 and 60 works for both choir and organ.

VIDEO | Our video/DVDs offer spiritual help, healing, and biblical guidance for a broad range of life issues including grief and loss, marriage, forgiveness, facing death, understanding suicide, bullying, addictions, Alzheimer's, and Christian formation.

Learn more about us at our website:
www.paracletepress.com
or phone us toll-free at 1.800.451.5006

SCAN
TO
READ